Chance The Rapper

FLYING HIGH TO SUCCESS, WEIRD AND INTERESTING FACTS ON CHANCELLOR JOHNATHAN BENNETT

Learn all about Chance The Rapper in 20 minutes

With Bern Bolo
The Bathroom Genius

Chance The Rapper

*

*

*

Flying High to Success

*

*

*

Weird and Interesting Facts on Chancellor Johnathan Bennett

By Bern Bolo

TABLE OF CONTENTS

***

- Introduction

- *He Once F**cked Up School* – Let's Get To Know Chance The Rapper

- *Chance The Rapper*: Another Chance For Music

- *Starting The Famous Life With Rapping*: Introducing The Famed Mixtapes And Collaborations

- *The Primero Uno*: The *'10 Day'* Mixtape

- Mixtape # 2: '*Acid Rap*'

- The Colorful Mixtape # 3: '*Coloring Book*'

- Collaboration Tape # 1: '*Surf*'

- Collab Tape #2: '*Free (Based Freestyles Mixtape)*'

- Collab Tape #3: '*Merry Christmas Lil' Mama*'

- *Chance The Rapper Talks About Life, The Chicago Music Scene, Smoking Weed, 'The Acid' And Pretty Much Anything About Him…*

- References

- Check Out Luke Bryan's Trivia!

INTRODUCTION

Oh hello, my beloved readers!

This next artist I'm about to talk about is earning so much because of his acquired talents in which people have been doubting at first. Let me introduce to you the artist I'm pertaining to!

It's Chance The Rapper, i's one of a hell of a rapper.....

*HE ONCE F**CKED UP SCHOOL* – LET's GET TO KNOW CHANCE THE RAPPER

He really did...

Well anyway, that was just a 'once upon a time' story because here's the real deal...

Chance The Rapper is actually a pretty clear name to have if you're a rapper. It's plainly taking out bits of letters from your first name and then adding the label "the rapper" by the end of it and then BAM!!! You could then be a worldwide renowned, sought-after rapper by the end of the first bus trip to Chicago!

But seriously, in Chance The Rapper's case... (*that's not the case...*)

Chance The Rapper who is born with the biological name Chancellor Johnathan Bennett is an American rapper, singer, actor and record producer from West Chatham, Chicago Illinois.

Chance grew up in a middle-class neighborhood in Chicago's south side and has always wanted to become a rapper.

Chance said that he had always been into rap since he was "super young". The first album he made was "The College Dropout" and he made it while he was in the fifth freaking grade! And ever since people started noticing his music and style, he then set his mark at rapping – because for him, this is what he wants to do.

His father – Ken Williams Bennet worked for the then former Senator Barack Obama. But according to daddy here, he always wanted his son Chance to be more of an 'office guy', you know... the men in uniform type? But as fate and destiny would really have it, we have to go by its course and become what is really destined for us. And for Chance, being a musician was really his fate.

But oh yes.... Sometimes, life plays somewhat like that little f**king fool at us and tempt and throw sh*t at us to not be able to see what's coming for us!

I hope you get that....

Yes, sometimes it does that but for the good reasons though because sometimes we also have to prove to ourselves and also to other people if we really deserve 'it'. And just like any other famous people who are now successfully living the luxurious and comfortable life... Chance also had his moments of life *"being a f**king fool throwing sh*t at us"*.

He has ultimately been challenged during high school days when he was already been dreaming of becoming a musician when even the people who were supposed to be called his "second parents", his teachers have not believed in his talents and capabilities that he would become one and be successful with this path. They truly ridiculed him.

And that was indeed shitty right?

And to make matters even worse for this young teen with lofty dreams –being suspended, f**king up his grades and eventually his whole school life because of the possession of illegal drugs specifically marijuana, so he had a 10-day suspension. But this would even... in a turn of events would even get best living crap out of him. And by I mean "the best"... I mean literally the best.

So I'm talking about a good kind of "crap" here since this suspension has somewhat become a blessing in disguise for him.

So see? Basically, this suspension (*which is indeed a bad thing*) has ironically turned things quite good for him!

How Ironic!!!

CHANCE THE RAPPER: ANOTHER CHANCE FOR MUSIC

So yes… he f*cked up school and the past wasn't very good to him, but because of these bad things that have happened, good karma has happened to him in return!

And the cat was right – *how ironic!*

That suspension has given him time to reflect on his deeds and for only 10 days, he has made his ultimate step-up plan and executed it flawlessly that it has taken him to wherever he exactly is right now, and that is stardom in the hip hop rap scene.

So in this time alone, he made the biggest prime breakthrough in his life and career – the making of his first full-length project the '*10 Day*' mixtape which is also known to many of his fans as '*#10Day*'.

Chance's '*10 Day*' mixtape has totally been his first album that took his whole life and eventually became his definite chance into pursuing his music until he came to that point to live. And that totals this mixtape which in here he talks about nostalgia, high school and much more. All about this famed rapper Chance The Rapper.

Don't worry, it's not grammatically wrong, nor it's redundancy – it's just that Chance, the rapper's stage name is Chance The Rapper.

Oh, I know you already get that or else you wouldn't have gotten this long reading his very clear-cut stage name…

Anyway… moving on!

STARTING THE FAMOUS LIFE WITH RAPPING: INTRODUCING THE FAMED MIXTAPES AND COLLABORATIONS

So you've already heard about Chancellor's journey into the music rap industry right? It was indeed a mixture of happiness, sadness and pretty much mixed emotions, but in the end is truly quite fulfilling right? It is certainly fulfilling because he got to where he is supposed to be.

He was only used to dreaming of becoming a rapper before - *he's even mocked by it!* But now, he is just in the right place to be in.

So after the breakthrough *'10 Day'* mixtape project, indeed a lot more mixtapes and even collaborations have followed.

And they are the following:

Mixtapes:

1. **'10 Day'** (*Of course, the one we've all been talking about...*)
2. **'Acid Rap'** (*The somewhat "progressed version" mixtape of '10 Day'*)
3. **'Coloring Book'** (*Now this is the "more progressed version" of the two mixtapes – it's even reviewed to be nominated for the Grammy's. That's how big deal this mixtape is!*)

Collaborations:

1. **'Surf'** *(with Donnie Trumpet & The Social Experiment)*
2. **'Free'** *(Based Freestyles Mixtape) (with Lil B)*
3. **'Merry Christmas Lil' Mama'** *(with Jeremih)*

THE PRIMERO UNO: THE *'10 DAY'* MIXTAPE

And so let us first settle this mixtape's controversies – well though I think it has already been settled as I have already detailed it to you awhile ago with Chance's own passage of words in the above pages.

Just feel free to scan back. (Wink!)

.

So anyway, this is the 'primero uno' – the first one of Chance The Rapper's mixtapes. It was released on April 3, 2012, an independent label and as a free digital download. The mixtape garnered significant buzz and critical acclaim and garnered the attention of many music media outlets. The mixtape has been streamed nearly 600,000 times and downloaded over 400,000 times on mixtape site DatPiff.

So this tape has 14 songs in the listing and here they are:

1. *"14,400 Minutes"*
2. *"Nostalgia"*
3. *"Missing You"*
4. *"Windows" (featuring Alex Wiley and Akenya Seymour)*
5. *"Brain Cells"*
6. *"Long Time"*
7. *"22Offs"*
8. *"U Got Me Fucked Up"*
9. *"Family" (featuring Vic Mensa and Sulaiman)*
10. *"Juke Juke"*
11. *"Fuck You Tahm Bout"*
12. *"Long Time II" (featuring Nico Segal)*
13. *"Prom Night"*
14. *"Hey Ma" (featuring Lili K. and Peter CottonTale)*

MIXTAPE # 2: 'ACID RAP'

And then came in the second mixtape entitled *'Acid Rap'*. The tape was introduced to the public on April 30, 2013, also as a free digital download.

By July 2013, the album debuted at number 63 on the *Billboard* Top R&B/Hip-Hop Albums, due to bootleg downloads on iTunes and Amazon not affiliated with the artist.

The mixtape has been certified "diamond" on a website for mixtapes named Datpiff, for garnering over a whopping million of downloads!

According to Chance The Rapper himself said this tape only continues to tell the story of his dedication to diversifying his sound while also furthering his growth as a lyricist and singer.

It also allowed him to get more involved the process of making music, leading to a richer musical landscape and collaborations with the likes of BJ The Chicago Kid and Black Hippy's Ab-Soul.

Chance spent a summer on tour with Childish Gambino while taking an "acid trip" to Mexico, and got co-signs from RZA, Action Bronson, ScHoolBoy Q, and a host of other vets in the Hip Hop/Rap industry.

He spoke with HipHopDX about growing up in Chicago, the scene as he sees it, his progression since *#10Day*, and what people can expect from this *'Acid Rap'* mixtape.

This mixtape is composed of 13 tracks which are detailed on the list below...

1. *"Good Ass Intro" (featuring BJ the Chicago Kid, Lili K., Kiara Lanier, Peter Cottontale, Will of the O'mys and JP of Kids These Days)*

2. *"Pusha Man / Paranoia" (featuring Lili K. and Nate Fox)*

3. *"Cocoa Butter Kisses" (featuring Vic Mensa and Twista)*

4. *"Juice"*

5. *"Lost" (featuring Noname)*

6. *"Everybody's Something" (featuring Saba and BJ the Chicago Kid)*

7. *"Interlude (That's Love)"*

8. *"Favorite Song" (featuring Childish Gambino)*

9. *"NaNa" (featuring Action Bronson)*

10. *"Smoke Again" (featuring Ab-Soul)*

11. *"Acid Rain"*

12. *"Chain Smoker"*

13. *"Everything's Good (Good Ass Outro)"*

THE COLORFUL MIXTAPE # 3: '*COLORING BOOK*'

And just a year after, this third one surely did get released as the third mixtape of Chance – the '*Coloring Book*' mixtape. And by this time, he is already labeled by many as one of the most talented rappers in his generation and a pioneer in the music industry.

Coloring Book," is one of the best-reviewed albums of the year and debuted at No. 8 on the Billboard 200 list (*pretty tight!*). It's the first streaming-only album to chart on Billboard's ranking.

So this mixtape is already undeniably successful, but the only catch is... he has successfully done all of this without a label supporting him!

Now I'm starting to think that irony is really a part of his life and that he is very good at it. Because come on! Can't you freaking see how ironic this is?!

Okay...........

HOW IRONIC – *AGAIN...*

He's turned down record deals from numerous labels and depends on word of mouth and his Soundcloud account for distribution. But yes, because irony has always favored this guy, what do you think happened next?

Yes... the mixtape turned to be an awesome deal for him, it was blasting successful and it was even considered as one of the best of that year so far! So see? No big deal...

This project is a 14-track playlist.

1. *"All We Got" (featuring Kanye West and Chicago Children's Choir)*
2. *"No Problem" (featuring Lil Wayne and 2 Chainz)*
3. *"Summer Friends" (featuring Jeremih and Francis and the Lights)*
4. *"D.R.A.M. Sings Special"*
5. *"Blessings"*
6. *"Same Drugs"*
7. *"Mixtape" (featuring Young Thug and Lil Yachty)*
8. *"Angels" (featuring Saba)*
9. *"Juke Jam" (featuring Justin Bieber and Towkio)*
10. *"All Night" (featuring Knox Fortune)*
11. *"How Great" (featuring Jay Electronica and My cousin Nicole)*
12. *"Smoke Break" (featuring Future)*
13. *"Finish Line / Drown" (featuring T-Pain, Kirk Franklin, Eryn Allen Kane and Noname)*
14. *"Blessings" (featuring Ty Dolla Sign, Raury, BJ the Chicago Kid and Anderson Paak)*

COLLABORATION TAPE # 1: 'SURF'

'Surf' is the debut studio collaboration album by American band The Social Experiment; where Chance The Rapper has also took part and is an active member. It was released exclusively on iTunes as a free download on May 28, 2015.

The album highlights a trumpeter by the name of Nico Segal, and was made possible by Segal along with his other band of collaborators called The Social Experiment — a self-described group of musicians, consisting of Donnie Trumpet, **Chance The Rapper**, Peter Cottontale, Greg Landfair Jr., Nate Fox and more.

So basically, this is not just Chance The Rapper alone.

Yes... yes... I can hear you now saying *"Of course he would not be the only one in this because it is obviously a collaboration album..."*

But know what??? Whatever... yeah smartass...

So anyway... The album's wide range of different artists also drew praise and attention to many but still, there are no official credited features listed in the iTunes track list.

And here below are the included songs in this intriguing project:

1. *"Miracle"*

2. *"Slip Slide"*

3. *"Warm Enough"*

4. *"Nothing Came to Me"*

5. *"Wanna Be Cool"*

6. *"Windows"*

7. *"Caretaker"*

8. *"Just Wait"*

9. *"Familiar"*

10. *"Smthnthtlwnt"*

11. *"Go"*

12. *"Questions"*

13. *"Something Came to Me"*

14. *"Rememory"*

15. *"Sunday Candy"*

16. *"Pass the Vibes"*

COLLAB TAPE #2: '*FREE (BASED FREESTYLES MIXTAPE)*'

'Free (Based Freestyles Mixtape)' is a collaborative mixtape by American rappers Chance the Rapper and the newly political Based God (*as he prefers to label himself*), the awesome - Lil B.

It was released for free on August 5, 2015.

It only has 6 tracks – *not much, though, but all are superb!*

I tried listening to the album's track titled "*Amen*" and all I could say was….

AMEN!!! OH LAWD HAVE MERCY THESE ARE A TASTE OF HEAVEN!

So here you go guys… try listening one of these yourself!

1. *"Last Dance"*
2. *"What's Next"*
3. *"First Mixtape"*
4. *"Amen"*
5. *"Do My Dance"*
6. *"We Rare"*

COLLAB TAPE #3: *'MERRY CHRISTMAS LIL' MAMA'*

And also then came in the 'Merry Christmas Lil' Mama' collaborative project. It is the fourth mixtape by Jeremih, and also the fourth mixtape by Chance the Rapper.

The mixtape was self-released by the group through SoundCloud on December 22, 2016, which featured collaborations with Hannibal Buress, King Louie and much more.

And for a small fun fact, this mixtape is dedicated to the city of Chicago.

And here are the 9 tracks on the album's listing…

1. *"All the Way"*
2. *"Snowed In"*
3. *"Stranger at the Table"*
4. *"Joy"*
5. *"I'm Your Santa"*
6. *"I Shoulda Left You"*
7. *"The Tragedy"*
8. *"Chi Town Christmas"*
9. *"Merry Christmas Lil' Mama"*

*CHANCE THE RAPPER TALKS ABOUT LIFE, THE CHICAGO MUSIC
SCENE, SMOKING WEED, 'THE ACID' AND PRETTY MUCH ANYTHING
ABOUT HIM...*

It has always been quite nice to know that we are gathering information especially someone's life details through their own tongue and words...

Of course... I don't want to get sued up or anything because I've been bogus on my explanations and the details here in my trivia are inadequate, so I have gathered these passages from Chance The Rapper's interviews about his life, the music industry, Chicago and even smoking weed.

So let's get it on!

Well, first of all, let's start by growing up in the Chicagoan neighborhood and what it was like for a Chancellor Bennett...

As for Chancelor, Chicago is indeed very good cultured City to grow up in. It has truly been a good base for him for his music. He even said that people could find a lot of music genres in the place, if you are only willing to find it, so it wasn't tough for him to adopt and finally learn the ways in music. There are also a lot of iconic artists who are from Chicago which he looks up to as well, like Kanye West and more – the history of the place is just as wonderful as its music, so he said that he certainly had a lot of things going on while growing in the "Windy City".

And when did he actually start his rapping:

Obviously, he started young. According to Chance, he had done some rhythms when he was still 14 years old. His cousin used to manage a recording studio back in Chicago, so as for him, it was a perfect timing to practice his skills. It was a big moment for him every time he does his music there because it was always his first time back then to listen to himself over some real tunes and according to him, he liked it! He kept his songs, but he said that it wasn't really for something big. He actually even shot a video for himself – his first ever suppose to be music video, but he really hopes nobody, that nobody, finds that sh*t.

I think it's that bad???

About the drugs, the weed and oh… *'THE ACID'* while working on with the mixtapes:

- Chancelor said and never denied that he uses these things to 'up' him up while making his music. According to him, it was his booster, and they were some good ones. (*Of course they were…*) He uses LSD actually. He said that towards the making of the album, while he was recording the songs, he used some weed. So he was officially '*high*' on drugs guys while making the tracks on his "*Acid Rap*" album – thus the album name "Acid Rap" was born since he called the tracks his '*acid raps*' while creating them successfully with weed.

And let us not forget the Chicago Music Scene, how is it:

Chancelor believes that the Chicago music scene is indeed the most influential and powerful music base these days. He said that until the drill music scene came out in the world, and that's actually when Chicago was out on the map. But as for him, people are more interested in tragedy and sadness apart from what's 'good'. And according to him – that sucked. And yes it does… but it was still kind of a good thing though, since artists who focus on this side of the coin, gets to come up on the ladder of success and at the same time, they too could tell their own story. And so, it was a win-win situation for them.

Are we expecting more from you? How about new labels:

Well…. Chance said that there might be a possibility soon, but as for now, they would still prefer to stay 'chillin'. Just him and his homies. Making music whenever he wants to without the pressure or busy schedules. Because as for him, labels would only spell a lot of partnership and many more variables. So he's chillin!

REFERENCES

https://en.wikipedia.org/wiki/Chance_the_Rapper

https://en.wikipedia.org/wiki/Chance_the_Rapper_discography

https://en.wikipedia.org/wiki/10_Day_(mixtape)

https://en.wikipedia.org/wiki/Acid_Rap

https://en.wikipedia.org/wiki/Coloring_Book_(mixtape)

https://en.wikipedia.org/wiki/Surf_(Donnie_Trumpet_%26_The_Social_Experiment_album)

https://en.wikipedia.org/wiki/Free_(Based_Freestyles_Mixtape)

https://en.wikipedia.org/wiki/Merry_Christmas_Lil%27_Mama

http://hiphopdx.com/interviews/id.2099/title.chance-the-rapper-talks-the-chicago-scene-his-acid-rap-mixtape#

https://mic.com/articles/131365/how-chance-the-rapper-went-from-high-school-fuckup-to-one-of-chicago-s-elite-artists#.SaS67X6Kq

http://www.businessinsider.com/chance-the-rapper-bio-history-2016-8/#chance-the-rapper-calls-his-albums-mixtapes-he-recorded-his-first-one-in-his-senior-year-of-high-school-1

http://www.gq.com/story/how-chance-the-rappers-life-became-perfect

http://www.aceshowbiz.com/celebrity/chance_the_rapper/biography.html

http://www.billboard.com/artist/4281953/chance-the-rapper/biography

http://www.thefamouspeople.com/profiles/chance-the-rapper-16144.php

http://chanceraps.com/

https://www.instagram.com/chancetherapper/?hl=en

Check Out Luke Bryan's Trivia!

Do you love country music? I'm not saying the 'Taylor Swift' type… the country music – the real deal! Well if you do, you'd be happy to know that this trivia isn't about Taylor Swift and her perfectly blonde hair and skinny body, but this is about a one-heart, true country man named Luke Bryan. His songs are amazing and not just that… here in this trivia, you'll discover what real country music through this guy's songs. You'll also learn here that some very tragic events can turn to gold and happiness in the long run, what it's like growing up in the country, how a once peanut-growing dad discovered his true son's talents and pursued him to do what he loves that led him to where he is today and MORE! Are you curious about these things? Click that button and buy it now or recommend it to your friends who love country music as much as I do.

Check Out Luke Bryan's Trivia
[Get your copy of Luke Bryan's Trivia!](#)

If you enjoyed this "Trivia", please leave an honest review on Amazon.com!

Sign-up here on [Bern Bolo's](#) site for Trivia On Twenty One Pilots!

www.ingramcontent.com/pod-product-compliance
Lightning Source LLC
Chambersburg PA
CBHW050921290526
45792CB00002B/843